Ivan Turgenev

by

CHARLES A. MOSER

 Columbia University Press

NEW YORK & LONDON

Copyright © 1972 Columbia University Press
ISBN: 0-231-03412-1
Library of Congress Catalog Card Number: 71-186640
Printed in the United States of America
9 8 7 6 5 4 3 2

Ivan Turgenev

Many critics now consider Ivan Turgenev the most dated of the great masters of the novel in nineteenth-century Russia. His exquisitely planned, finely wrought books are "faded," they say; the political issues which concerned him have long since lost their immediacy; his approach is sentimental, even mawkish; he supplies nourishment only to "those who find meat and drink in clouds and nymphs," in the words of an unkind contemporary scholar. So runs the standard list of complaints about the most civilized and cosmopolitan of Russian writers. And indeed there is some truth in them. Turgenev cannot boast the verbal exuberance and astounding inventiveness of a Gogol, the profound energy and conviction of a Dostoevsky wrestling with problems of a sort which our age thinks very relevant, the epic sweep of description and inquiry to be found in Tolstoy, the painstaking attention to detail and psychological analysis of a Goncharov. Yet despite all this, Turgenev displays strengths which led that American original Albert Jay Nock to call him "incomparably the greatest of artists in fiction"—or Virginia Woolf to describe his books as "curiously of our own time, undecayed, and complete in themselves"—and which ensure that he will continue to be read both in his native country and in the West for as long as we can foresee. The intellectual fashions may be against him at the moment and may remain so for some time, but Turgenev has never been totally eclipsed, and such a fate is scarcely likely to befall him in the near future.

Turgenev wrote primarily brief novels and short stories. He was a master of literary form and a superb stylist, with a com-

[3]

mand of the Russian language which was the envy of his contemporaries. His skill at painting with words, especially in his nature descriptions, has never been surpassed. Turgenev was a genuine literary professional. As he was independently wealthy, he had time to polish his efforts, for he did not depend upon literature for his living (an economic reason for the inordinate length of many Russian novels is that Russian writers of the nineteenth century were paid according to the number of pages they produced). He watched the contemporary political scene closely, and any reader who wishes to obtain a detailed understanding of Russian intellectual and political life of the mid-nineteenth century is well advised to read Turgenev. Turgenev was a subtle student of human psychology, especially as it manifests itself in the relationships between men and women. He was concerned with the great questions of life and death, too, and although his responses to them were shallower than those of Dostoevsky or Tolstoy, much more akin to those of Lermontov before him or Chekhov after him, it remains true that to study Turgenev carefully is to gain a fuller appreciation of life. Such strong points as these guarantee that, for all his weaknesses, Turgenev will continue to occupy a secure niche in the pantheon of his country's greatest authors.

Ivan Sergeevich Turgenev was born on October 28, 1818, in the town of Orel, located in the heartland of Russia. Orel was not far from the Turgenev family estate at Spasskoe, which later became the writer's principal Russian retreat. His mother, who evidently loved to dominate those under her authority, repelled the young Ivan by her cruelty to her serfs. His handsome father, who died in 1834, was content to let his wife manage the estate while he pursued local females more attractive to him than his spouse. After 1827, for the greater part of the year the family resided in Moscow, only returning to

[4]

Spasskoe in the summers. Thus from childhood Turgenev was intimately acquainted with the Russian country estate, that small fiefdom which could be culturally and economically almost independent, and which he made the setting for much of his later fiction.

Turgenev was first educated at Moscow boarding schools, then tutored at home, in the best tradition of the Russian gentry, for several years before he entered Moscow University in the fall of 1833. Moscow University was, intellectually speaking, the place to be at that juncture. An entire generation of talented men, including the poet Mikhail Lermontov, the novelist Ivan Goncharov, the journalist and revolutionary Alexander Herzen, the radical poet Nikolai Ogarev, and the critic Vissarion Belinsky, found spiritual sustenance there — sometimes within the lecture halls, more often outside them, in student "circles" of their own. Moscow University nurtured the great intellectual generation of the 1840s in Russia, many of whose members had had their careers terminated or interrupted by 1850, though not before they had bestowed their impress upon Russian intellectual life. Despite this, Turgenev soon elected to desert Moscow for St. Petersburg University, arriving just in time to attend lectures in world history given there by Gogol and graduating in 1837, at the age of eighteen.

Never again would Turgenev spend as many as eighteen years uninterruptedly in his homeland. In the spring of 1838, feeling that his undergraduate days had given him no more than the bare rudiments of an education, he set out for the source, the University of Berlin. Thus began his lifelong odyssey through Europe. From September, 1838, to September, 1839, Turgenev spent most of his time in Berlin, following the latest in German philosophy and gaining entrance to the world of Teutonic culture. But it was also in Berlin that he met that semi-legendary embodiment of Russian culture of the time, Nikolai Stankevich.

[5]

Stankevich, who has come down to us as the prototype of the pure, idealistic Russian intellectual of the 1830s, died an untimely death at twenty-seven in 1840, only a short while after he and Turgenev had met again, this time in Rome, and become close friends. Turgenev has left us a highly spiritualized portrait of him in the character of Pokorsky from the novel *Rudin.* It was also in 1840, and again in Berlin, that Turgenev made the acquaintance of the famous anarchist Mikhail Bakunin. Their mutual interest in German philosophy created a tight though short-lived bond between them, and one which spawned embarrassing consequences when Turgenev visited Bakunin's multitudinous brothers and sisters for a few weeks at the end of 1841: a sister of Bakunin's fell extravagantly in love with him, and he extricated himself from the situation only with some difficulty. His reluctance to become involved with Bakunin's sister did not spring from any antipathy toward women: he had evidently been introduced to sex early on by a peasant girl, and just at the end of 1841 another peasant girl at Spasskoe was carrying his daughter Pauline, born in the spring of 1842. Turgenev saw to her upbringing, and in the 1860s succeeded in marrying her off to a French businessman despite her illegitimate origins.

Affairs of the heart did not overwhelm the life of the mind, however. Turgenev spent the academic year 1840-41 at the University of Berlin, and in the spring of 1842 took his examinations for the degree of Master of Philosophy at St. Petersburg University. From 1842 through 1847 he lived chiefly in St. Petersburg, though he took several trips to Moscow, Spasskoe, and Western Europe.

The year 1843 saw the initiation of two relationships which were perhaps the most fateful of Turgenev's life, with the critic Vissarion Belinsky and the singer Pauline Viardot. Although he had known Belinsky's articles for some time, Turgenev first

[6]

met the foremost Russian critic of the nineteenth century, that man "exceptionally dedicated to truth," as he put it in his reminiscences written twenty-five years later, in the summer of 1843. The two subsequently spent long hours in philosophical discussion of great intensity: Turgenev later recalled that when he once interrupted a conversation of theirs to wonder about dinner, Belinsky remonstrated with him quite seriously, "We haven't yet decided the question of God's existence, and you want to eat!" Just as he had done with Stankevich, Turgenev spent time with the mortally ill Belinsky in Salzbrunn in 1847, less than a year before Belinsky died of tuberculosis in St. Petersburg at the age of thirty-seven.

Turgenev's connection with Pauline Viardot, one of the most famous singers of her day, was of a different sort. In 1840 she had married Louis Viardot, an art historian and critic some twenty years her elder. She met Turgenev while on tour in Moscow in 1843, at which point there began one of the most extraordinary *ménage à trois* arrangements in the history of literature. From then until 1883, a span of forty years, Turgenev's thoughts were rarely far from her, and for great periods of time he lived near the Viardots. The three were almost inseparable, and Turgenev and Louis Viardot died within months of each other. Turgenev's attachment to Pauline Viardot (it may possibly have been platonic) prevented him from ever thinking seriously of marrying. In a way he possessed a complete family, but his "wife" was bound to another man, and his daughter was the offspring of a woman he cared nothing for. All in all, the situation seems hardly satisfactory.

In the St. Petersburg period of his life between 1842 and 1847 Turgenev did not keep at any very definite formal employment for long. Most of his energies were devoted to literature. His first immature effort, the dramatic poem "Steno" (1834), had been composed in verse, the dominant vehicle of the 1830s.

[7]

But his initial serious effort, the narrative poem "Parasha," dated from 1843 and was subtitled "A Short Story in Verse," in an obvious reference to the subtitle of Pushkin's *Eugene Onegin*, "A Novel in Verse." Belinsky dedicated a lengthy article to "Parasha," commending it warmly for being composed in "splendid poetic verse" and "imbued with a profound idea and completeness of inner content." For some time Turgenev continued to work the same vein, producing such narrative poems as "A Conversation" (1843) and "The Landowner" (1845), in addition to a quantity of lyric poems. Simultaneously, however, he tried his hand in other areas, for example plays and some short stories in prose, especially "Andrey Kolosov" of 1844, in which the narrator generously resolves to take up a girl jilted by one of his best friends, only to discover that when she responds to his overtures he loses interest and shame-facedly drops her too. It is clear that in his earliest stories and poems Turgenev has already treated the chief themes of his career, most especially that of love gone awry. This fact has been obscured to some extent, however, by the fact that toward the end of the 1840s he made a slight but significant detour in his literary development. The first hint of this was the appearance in 1847 of the initial sketch of those which eventually constituted *A Hunter's Notes*.

This piece, "Khor and Kalinych," was subtitled "From a Hunter's Notes" by an editor and tucked away in the miscellaneous section of *The Contemporary,* the leading literary journal of the day. In it the author, with great richness of detail and psychological skill, delineated the distinct and contrasting personalities of two serfs. Each is shown as a full and interesting human being, and each is shown—so subtly as to make it seem almost incidentally—as weighed down by his servile status and unconvinced that his lot has genuinely improved of late. This story, along with a few others published by the

[8]

end of 1847, caused Belinsky to conclude that Turgenev's future lay precisely along the lines of the hunting sketches, rather than those of his early poetry. If the critic was not wholly right in this estimate, he was entirely correct in remarking that a "chief characteristic" of Turgenev's talent was his inability "accurately to create a character whose like he had not encountered in reality," that reality must always serve as Turgenev's touchstone.

Though the sketches in *A Hunter's Notes* have remained among Turgenev's highest achievements, they are not the most typical of his works, for later on he reverted to the type of story illustrated by "Andrey Kolosov." For the time being, however, he accepted Belinsky's prescription, publishing further peasant sketches individually and then collecting them in 1852 under the general title *A Hunter's Notes* (a final three were added as late as 1874). In his last years Turgenev used to congratulate himself upon the contribution his book had made to the emancipation of the serfs in 1861. And indeed his claim was probably substantial. The book made a solid political point while not ceasing to be art.

The chief thrust of *A Hunter's Notes* as a whole continued to be that of depicting peasants as human beings, but human beings diminished by an officially sanctioned system of enslavement. The peasant boys in "Bezhin Meadow" who sit about a fire of an evening telling one another frightening tales, Kasyan with his pungent personality in "Kasyan of Krasivaya Mecha," Khor and Kalinych, all are unforgettable portraits. The reader also remembers the almost unconscious cruelty of the landowners who are accustomed to giving their serfs short shrift: "The way I see it, if you're a master then be a master; if you're a peasant than be a peasant," one of them says in "Two Landowners." However, it would be an error to think of the entire collection as structured around a contrast between admirable peasants and bestial landowners. Some landowners, though perhaps feckless, are depicted as genuinely interested in their peasants' welfare, and the serfs are often drawn as not particularly honest (Turgenev noted as one of their main characteristics a tendency to lie purely for the sake of lying) and occasionally downright repulsive, as in the scene of the drunken, swinish peasants at the conclusion of "The Singers." Moreover, the author is interested in a number of things with no direct bearing upon social relationships: he transmits the folk beliefs of the common people, or investigates the manner in which individuals face the immediate prospect of death ("A Country Doctor" is a poignant story of a lonely, incompetent doctor who falls deeply in love with a dying girl whom he cannot save). Turgenev is also concerned with aesthetic matters: he gives an extraordinarily detailed description of the singing competition in "The Singers," and the thing most readers remember from the welter of detail—the quantity of detail which makes it difficult to recall the outline of any particular story is perhaps the book's main weakness—is his magnificent nature descriptions. The final sketch, "Forest and Steppe," consists entirely of unsurpassed lyrical word-painting.

Turgenev's best-known single story dedicated to the unfortunate condition of the serfs was "Mumu" of 1852, not included in *A Hunter's Notes*. Much anthologized in the Soviet Union today because of its relatively overt social criticism, the tale describes the hard lot of a deaf and dumb servant who for lack of any other object forms an attachment to a dog, but has even this small solace taken from him through the unheeding cruelty of his captious, elderly female owner. The hero, Gerasim, is drawn as a very positive character despite the physical affliction which makes him a trifle peculiar and for which no one can be held responsible; but few of those around him, including his fellow serfs, make any effort to ease his situation. His position would have been trying enough had he been a free man, but the far-reaching powers over him granted to his owner by the institution of serfdom certainly intensified his misfortunes. "Mumu" stands as Turgenev's most forthright indictment of the system of serfdom.

Over the years when the stories in *A Hunter's Notes* were appearing, Turgenev pursued other tacks as well. In 1849, while living abroad, he wrote a work of cardinal importance for all Russian literature, "The Diary of a Superfluous Man." The phrase "superfluous man" has since become the mightiest cliché in the criticism of nineteenth-century Russian literature, utilized as it now is to link Pushkin's Onegin, Lermontov's Pechorin, Goncharov's Oblomov, and several other literary creations as essentially positive characters unjustly treated by contemporary society. But it was Turgenev who through his story gave the phrase its first wide currency, even though his hero, Chulkaturin, is more psychologically than socially or politically superfluous. The work is cast in the form of a diary kept by Chulkaturin in the last days before his death, which occurs on April Fool's Day, appropriately enough. Though the consciousness of his impending demise weighs upon both Chulkaturin and the reader, Turgenev underlines the complete indifference of nature toward the fortunes of her creatures, of whom man is only one: there is a constant and jarring discord between the budding life of the incipient spring in which the narrative is set and Chulkaturin's morbid sickliness. Chulkaturin is a sensitive though excessively self-conscious individual, capable of analyzing himself as well as others with impressive penetration. This is especially the case now, when he is summing up his life, as it were; but at the same time he realizes that in the actual situations he looks back on he either acted totally inappropriately or misinterpreted the deeds and attitudes of others. The most central of Chulkaturin's characteristics is his

[11]

"superfluity," his quality of always being a "supernumerary." "Evidently nature had not counted on my putting in an appearance," he says, "and therefore treated me like an uninvited and unexpected guest. . . . All during the course of my life I constantly found my place already occupied, perhaps because I looked for that place where I should not have." The narrative illustrates this apparently almost fated trait of his life: he has hopes of winning the love of a young lady but is frustrated by the appearance of a dashing prince who wins her heart instead; when he attempts to defend her honor he merely earns her hatred; at the end he "magnanimously" resolves to cover for her sins, only to discover that yet another rival has preceded him. Nothing remains for him but to acquiesce first in his own humiliation, then in his own dissolution. Chulkaturin is an outstanding literary creation: he is both sufficiently individualized and sufficiently generalized to endure in the treasury of world literature.

Given Turgenev's general literary approach, one might expect him to be interested in writing for the stage, and indeed for a time it seemed he might leave a large body of dramatic writing. Beginning with a brief piece in a Spanish setting dating from 1843, Turgenev produced some ten plays of varying length before abandoning the genre permanently after 1852, largely for extraliterary reasons: the theatrical censorship at the time was unusually strict, so that Turgenev despaired of even getting his plays published, much less staged. And later on, when the situation improved, he somehow failed to try his hand at the drama again.

Turgenev's finest play—one which remains a staple of the Russian repertory to this day and is often presented on Western stages as well—is *A Month in the Country*, written in 1850. A play of Chekhovian mood created long before Chekhov was born, it is based on a situation reminiscent of Turgenev's own

[12]

relationship with the Viardot family. The hero, Rakitin, is a freeloader and devotee of the lady of the house, whose husband is too preoccupied with managing the estate to pay her much heed. However, Rakitin is also an educated man with a morbid sensitivity to the beauties of nature. The world of the estate — outwardly idyllic but inwardly full of discontent and potential unhappiness — is disturbed by the arrival of a young tutor, whose unaffected naturalness and energy awaken the love of both the jaded mistress of the estate, Natalya Petrovna, and her seventeen-year-old ward, Vera. Rakitin follows the situation almost as an external observer and, though at first incredulous, soon realizes that the only solution is for both him and the tutor, Belyaev, to take their leave. Rakitin then departs for the future of a lonely bachelor, Belyaev leaves for the more important things he presumably has the capacity to achieve, Vera escapes what has become an intolerable situation at home by accepting the proposal of a kind but dull man thirty years her elder, and Natalya Petrovna subsides into the rut of existence on her husband's well-managed estate. Thus the tutor's brief stay on the estate precipitates a whole series of crises: the situation of the characters at the end is very different from what it was at the beginning, and the majority of them are worse off than before. The entire piece is imbued with an autumnal atmosphere: everyone's situation is somehow out of joint, and there are no real prospects for improvement. *A Month in the Country* encountered difficulties with censorship: it could be published only in modified form, with Natalya Petrovna a widow rather than a wife, in 1855, and not in its original version until 1869.

The period during which Turgenev established his literary reputation was not a propitious one for Russian literature: the years 1848 to 1855, from the European revolutions to the death of Czar Nichoas I, are now called the "Epoch of Censorship

Terror." Herzen, sensing what was below the horizon, left his homeland in 1847 never to return; Belinsky died an early death in 1848; Dostoevsky was exiled to Siberia for subversive activities in 1849. During this period Belinsky's name could not be mentioned in print and any hint of disloyal intent was blue-penciled by the censors. At first Turgenev was not especially affected by these conditions. Between 1847 and 1850 he traveled extensively in Western Europe, particularly France and Germany, and though he may have been regarded by some in the government as a carrier of the revolutionary virus, nothing untoward happened to him until 1852. Then, ironically enough, he suffered for writing an obituary extolling Gogol, politically the most conservative of the great Russian writers, whom Belinsky had attacked scathingly not long before his own death. But evidently the government did not care to see any writers praised, and Turgenev was jailed in St. Petersburg for a month, though not under very arduous conditions, for his friends could visit him freely and his meals were brought to him from the outside. Thereafter, from May, 1852, to November, 1853, he was exiled to Spasskoe, which he had inherited after his mother's death in 1850, returning to the capital only at the very end of 1853.

The year 1855 saw the opening of a new era in the history of nineteenth-century Russia. When the country was far along toward losing the Crimean War, Nicholas I, remembered as the greatest tyrant among the Czars, was succeeded by Alexander II, the "Czar-Liberator," who decreed the emancipation of the serfs in 1861. The beginning of Alexander's reign was a period of high hopes: it saw the lightening of the censorship and a resultant quickening of intellectual life. In addition, the 1850s witnessed a transition from the philosophical idealism of the 1840s to the politically radical activism of the 1860s. If the

[14]

first half of the decade was a period of stagnation, the second was a time of ideological reorientation. It was then that the consistent old-line liberal Turgenev noted the first hints of trouble from those to his political left. This occurred when *The Contemporary*, under the editorship of his old friend Nikolai Nekrasov, began a process of radicalization under the guidance of the radical critics Nikolai Chernyshevsky and Nikolai Dobrolyubov. Chernyshevsky and Dobrolyubov were impatient with Turgenev's absorption with what they considered trivial affairs of the heart at a time when all honorable people should have been worrying about political and social problems. Turgenev never denied the importance of social problems, but at the same time he defended the artist's independence and his right to deal with other subjects he felt were also significant. Chernyshevsky and Dobrolyubov gradually took Nekrasov along with them, and after they had insulted Turgenev irreparably, the latter broke with both *The Contemporary* and Nekrasov.

By the end of the 1850s Turgenev was famous as the "great poet of the doomed love affair," to use Alfred Kazin's phrase of a later date. "Faust" (1856), a "Short Story in Nine Letters," displays several major themes in Turgenev's writing: the potentially malign influence of artistic literature upon the minds of people unprepared to cope with it; an awareness of the supernatural intervening in human life; the violent, sudden snatching of the fruits of love from between outstretched hands: "What there was between us flashed by instantaneously, like lightning, and like lightning bore death and destruction." Some years after their first acquaintance the hero of "Faust" meets the heroine, now married to a pedestrian husband. Though the heroine's late mother had strictly forbidden her ever to read fiction, the hero, who could never comprehend the reason for this prohibition, begins to visit her estate and recite *Faust* to her. The poem

[15]

wreaks such a change in her character that the relationship between hero and heroine develops to the stage where each avows love for the other. On her way to the assignation which would have led to the consummation of their passion, however, the heroine is stopped by her mother's apparition. She returns home with a mysterious ailment to which she succumbs in two weeks, leaving the hero to the standard lonely future.

Just as in "Faust," artistic literature, represented in this instance by Pushkin's foreboding lyric "The Upas-Tree," plays a crucial role in the story "A Quiet Spot" (1854). A brief work which took Turgenev six months to compose, it is not particularly successful, partly because of the excessive number of plot lines but primarily because the heroine's character is delineated so sketchily that her final decisive act of committing suicide seems insufficiently motivated. The reader may surmise, however, that she is designed as a deeply passionate though disciplined soul compelled to live among potential or actual philistines, and that the impression made upon her mind, so unaccustomed to artistic literature, by her reading of Pushkin's poem triggers her fatal decision.

In his love stories of the 1850s Turgenev rang the changes on the basic theme of the abrupt denial of love's fruits. "Asya," for example, written in Rome at the end of 1857 after the author had weathered a spiritual crisis, may be viewed as one of the most characteristic of Turgenev's love stories. The tale is set in Germany rather than on a Russian estate, but the foreign environment serves primarily to bring the Russian characters— the narrator N., Gagin, and the latter's illegitimate half-sister Asya—closer together than they might have been in a native setting. A consuming love sweeps over the heroine, reducing her to a state of physical illness. But when she offers her love to N. during the climactic scene, where he must accept or reject her on the spot, he declines to do either, but instead temporizes wordily. To be sure, he quickly realizes his error and within twelve hours is prepared to grasp the opportunity presented him, but he is too late: the Gagins depart and he is unable to trace them. At the time he consoles himself with the thought that other opportunities may present themselves, but he is wrong: "Condemned to the loneliness of an old bachelor, I live out my dull years, but I preserve as something sacred her little notes and a faded geranium, the same blossom she threw me from the window once upon a time."

"First Love," a long short story of 1860, is among the most autobiographical of Turgenev's writings, being based in large measure on the situation in his own family, with his philandering father married to an unattractive and older woman. As was the case with "Asya," the story is recalled through the prism of intervening years by a hero for whom the events described were crucial; the impressions are those of a youth of sixteen not fully cognizant of what is happening about him, as recalled and interpreted by an older man. The narrator describes his first passion for a beautiful but impoverished princess, Zinaida, a capricious and independent young woman completely dominant over her suite of admirers, but who submits to the narrator's father, a man who values independence and freedom above all. The reader must take some pains to piece together the history of the love affair between Zinaida and the father, for the narrator himself perceived it only fragmentarily, being most concerned with his own emotions upon first falling in love. And certainly the story is a masterpiece of psychological analysis in its description of the reactions of a boy in this state who realizes that he faces a successful rival in his own father, whom he greatly admires. But even successful love engenders disaster: the father dies of a stroke soon after the affair is terminated,

[17]

leaving as a legacy the words, "My son, fear woman's love; fear that happiness, that poison"; Zinaida, after bearing an illegitimate child, makes the best marriage she can but dies a mere four years later. In "First Love," as in many of Turgenev's other works, love is like a disease which can result only in damage: it ruins one's life if unrequited, it ruins one's life if requited. The temporary joys it brings must be paid for in excessive measure.

Turgenev is now remembered as a novelist, though, even more than as a short-story writer. Although he did not get around to separating his novels from his short stories until 1880, Turgenev wrote a total of six of them: *Rudin, On the Eve, A Nest of Gentlefolk, Fathers and Sons, Smoke,* and *Virgin Soil.* His novels differ from his short stories in that the latter deal primarily with personal emotions and love conflicts, whereas the former also treat broader social questions. However, even in the novels Turgenev's interest remained focused upon his heroes' distinct personalities. He once remarked that he always began from a personality rather than an abstract idea, and thus it is not surprising to find him supplying his heroes with detailed pre-histories either in his notes for a novel or in the novel itself, and setting them very carefully in historical context. Another hallmark of Turgenev as literary artist was the externalizing of his characters' psychology. He rejected Tolstoy's method of analyzing his heroes' psychological motives directly and at length. The artist, he held, should be a "secret psychologist": Turgenev knows quite as well as Tolstoy how his heroes think and feel, but he causes them to express their internal experience through words and external actions, so that the reader must deduce their inner feelings from outward signs, just as in real life. To be sure, Turgenev's characters occasionally deliver themselves of monologues which are more closely allied to Tolstoy's approach, but on the whole the reader is presented with a substantial task of interpretation in dealing with Turgenev's writing.

A famous article of Turgenev's, published in 1859 under the title "Hamlet and Don Quixote," is worth considering briefly as a key to his view of life and literature. In this piece Turgenev postulated the Hamlet-type and the Quixote-type as polar opposites among human characters. To Turgenev's mind, Don Quixote represents primarily "faith," "faith in truth located beyond the individual." The Don dedicates his entire life to a cause outside himself. This makes him appear mad to some, and it indisputably bestows a considerable monotony upon his mind: "he knows little, but he does not have to know much." At the same time, he is "the most moral creature in the world," this insane knight. Hamlet is quite his opposite: he represents "analysis first of all, and egotism, and therefore lack of faith." Though an egotist, Hamlet is simultaneously too skeptical to believe in himself. Though intelligent, he finds his own internal resources insufficient. His weapon is irony, where Don Quixote's is enthusiasm. Don Quixote would not fear to seem foolish in the eyes of the world, whereas Hamlet thinks there is nothing worse than this. Hamlet despises this life and wishes he could end it, but he is still too much attached to it to make any serious attempt to do so. Turgenev does remind us, though, that Hamlet suffers much more intensely than Don Quixote: the latter undergoes only physical discomfort inflicted by others, whereas Hamlet tortures himself spiritually.

The first of Turgenev's novels, *Rudin*, contains a central hero constructed largely on the pattern of Hamlet. Composed in six or seven weeks during the summer of 1855 at Spasskoe, it was published early the following year in *The Contemporary* and in a separate edition a few months later. The story is laid in yet another isolated Russian estate, where Rudin appears abruptly and unexpectedly. When he leaves a short time later, every-

[19]

thing remains outwardly much as it was before, but inward tensions have been created which will markedly alter the fortunes of the individuals in the group Rudin finds there. This group includes Darya Mikhaylovna, the imperious and vain mistress of the estate; her daughter, Natalya, the book's heroine; a neighboring landowner, Volyntsev, who at first refrains from making an open avowal of his love for Natalya but who eventually wins her as his wife; the sycophant and secret sensualist Pandalevsky; the embittered misogynist and poseur Pigasov; and the earnest tutor Basistov. All of these are affected in one way or another by Rudin, especially by his flair for rhetoric, the "music of his eloquence." Words are Rudin's stock in trade. "Some of his hearers very likely did not understand precisely what he was talking about," the author comments, "but his breast heaved, some sort of curtains were withdrawn before his eyes, and something radiant flared up before him." After listening to him for a time Darya Mikhaylovna calls him a "poet," and Turgenev emphasizes the fact that Rudin is often carried away by the music of his own eloquence, in what is indeed a rather poetic fashion.

Rudin almost desperately uses words as a cover for his lack of inner emotion. Toward the end of the novel one character remarks that "Rudin has the nature of a genius," only to be corrected by another: "There is a touch of genius in him, . . . but nature—that's the whole thing, he really has no nature." There lies within Rudin an emotional void which he strives to fill with words and intellectual convictions, but cannot. He is a man lacking in passion who feels that he should be passionate. But his predilection for intellectual analysis and verbalization destroys any possibility of true emotional commitment. In his student days he wrecked a love affair in which one of his friends was involved by insisting on analyzing it and informing other

[20]

people about it. In the novel he does the same thing to his own love affair: when Natalya offers herself to him without reservations, he knows he should respond but can feel nothing. He therefore attempts to counterfeit the appropriate emotions, but fails, and afterwards loses Natalya because he cannot take positive action at the time required. He tries to justify his failure in a lengthy analytic letter written to her when he leaves, but words simply cannot compensate for his lack of substance. At the end of the novel as orginally published, Rudin is depicted dejectedly and aimlessly wandering through Russia.

Apparently, though, Turgenev was uncomfortable over leaving his hero in such an existential limbo, for in 1860 he took the unusual step of adding to the novel an epilogue presenting him in a slightly more favorable light. Rudin himself tells of several projects which he had undertaken but which had all come to naught because of his inability to accomplish anything practical. At the same time, he is reconciled with his old university classmate, who had been very much against him during the body of the novel; and the author grants that the uttering of the right words at the right time may be a form of action. At the end, in a scene whose appropriateness is open to some question, Turgenev brings Rudin to the Parisian barricades of June, 1848, and there has him perish, shot through the heart, after the revolution has already been put down. Thus in the final accounting he does prove capable of action, though fate decrees that even this shall be abortive.

Turgenev had been planning his second novel, *A Nest of Gentlefolk*, as early as 1856, but circumstances prevented serious work on it before a sojourn at Spasskoe in 1858. The book was written in the latter half of that year and published in early 1859 (publication early in the year is a nearly constant pattern with Turgenev's novels). Though *A Nest of Gentlefolk* was received by contemporaries with approbation, its popularity has not stood the test of time well, and it is now among the least read of his novels.

In the years immediately following 1855 Turgenev was for some reason at his most Slavophile or Russophile. Toward the conclusion of *Rudin* he had caused a character for whom he obviously felt some sympathy to make a strong statement against cosmopolitanism and to define the source of Rudin's unhappiness as his ignorance of Russia. "Russia can get along without us," he says, "but none of us can get along without her. Woe to him who thinks he can, and double woe to him who actually does!" In *A Nest of Gentlefolk* Turgenev continued to work along lines such as these. This should not be taken to mean that he abandoned his Western predilections, but he did at that time look most sympathetically on the Russian traits of his heroes and most unfavorably upon certain aspects of Western culture. This is exemplified by the history of the father of the book's hero, Lavretsky. The father was a scatterbrained Anglophile who tried to bring Lavretsky up as a rootless European. However, not only does Lavretsky rediscover the values of his native land in the good sense, but his father is transformed into a Russian in the bad sense when he suddenly goes blind, wanders across Russia seeking a cure, and dies a crotchety Russian landowner of the classical type. Aside from this, in *A Nest of Gentlefolk* Turgenev also devotes a great deal of attention to the problem of the family as the foundation stone of any society. He provides Lavretsky with the most extensive family history of any of his major characters, tracing his ancestors back several centuries and dwelling in much more detail than was usual even for him on Lavretsky's immediate family. In like manner, the "nest" of the title is a family nest depicted in loving detail at the end of the book. Lavretsky has nothing to do with its existence, but he appreciates the principle of human continuity which it embodies.

Lavretsky himself is a likable man with scholarly inclinations who is trapped between two women representing the poles of womankind in Turgenev's fiction. His wife, Varvara Pavlovna, is unredeemable: she exploits her husband, is blithely unfaithful to him with insignificant men, makes demands upon him when she has nowhere else to turn, and generally blights his life. She is one of several heroines in Turgenev who feed their egos by exercising power over men. For a time, misled by a false report of her death in Paris where he has left her in order to return to Russia, Lavretsky is deceived into thinking he can find true happiness with the book's heroine, Liza, the most ethereal, most moral, and strongest-willed of Turgenev's women. Intensely religious, Liza is disturbed by the notion of loving a man promised to another woman, even if the latter be dead. In a brief scene of suppressed passion, the two seem on the verge of happiness until all this is suddenly destroyed by the reappearance of Varvara Pavlovna. Liza interprets the return of Lavretsky's wife as divine punishment for her spiritual insolence and resolves to take up life as a nun in a distant convent. Lavretsky is soon abandoned by his wife once again. The novel ends with a vignette describing Lavretsky's visit years later to Liza's convent. As he watches her pass by a few feet from him, "only the lashes of the eye turned toward him trembled slightly, she merely bent her emaciated face lower—and the fingers of her clasped hands, intertwined with prayer beads, clenched more tightly." In these external signs may be read the extent of Liza's inner strength.

One of the most dynamic male characters Turgenev ever created was Insarov, the Bulgarian hero of his third novel, *On the Eve*. The author began the book in the summer of 1859 while taking the waters at Vichy, although he had been nurturing the idea for it since 1855, when a friend had given him a manuscript describing an unfortunate love between a Bulgarian man and a Russian girl. Completed in the autumn at Spasskoe, it appeared in the January, 1860, issue of the *Russian Herald*, the journal in which Turgenev would publish for some years following his break with *The Contemporary* despite its conservative politics and his general dislike for its editor, Mikhail Katkov.

On the Eve sharply contrasts the Russian male—in the persons of Shubin, an artist of ability and intelligence but lacking in constancy, and Bersenev, a good man and a scholar who ends by producing articles on such trivial topics as "On Certain Peculiarities of Ancient German Law in the Matter of Judicial Punishments"—and the dedicated Russian female in the character of Elena Stakhova. The single-minded Bulgarian Insarov is the only one who can satisfy her aspirations and meet her standards. Having grown up untamed by her family, Elena has reached just the right age for love when she first meets Insarov, at that time a student in Moscow in the period preceding the outbreak of the Crimean War in 1853. Insarov is totally devoted to the goal of freeing his country from its Turkish occupiers, and it is this complete dedication which makes him one of the most Don Quixote-like characters in Turgenev's fiction. The analytical Shubin presents the major traits of Insarov's character admirably in two sculptures he does of him. The first is a realistic bust in which his features are "honorable, noble, and bold," but the second depicts him as a rearing ram in whose countenance are expressed "dull pomposity, fervor, stubbornness, clumsiness, and narrowness." But the first Insarov is the one who remains predominantly in the reader's mind and the one who inspired Dobrolyubov to write his famous article

"When Will the Real Day Come?" in which he lauded Insarov while at the same time looking to the appearance of his Russian counterpart in the near future.

Once Insarov and Elena meet the plot develops rapidly. Elena takes the initiative in pressing her love upon him. Though he knows a revolutionary should have no family ties, he takes her when she agrees to accept his cause wholly and make no demands of her own on him. She thereupon abandons her family and Russia to go with her husband to Bulgaria to fight for liberation. Evidently, however, the couple have upset the balance of fate by their actions. Insarov contracts an illness while attempting to make arrangements for his wife to accompany him. He recovers, but falls ill again in Vienna and finally in Venice, where he dies before regaining his native soil. It is Insarov himself who raises the question of whether his illness is not punishment, and perhaps it is—a sign that personal happiness cannot be combined with dedication to a political cause. Then too, Insarov is a prime example of his creator's belief that if a man of action appears on the scene before history is ripe for him (after all, the Crimean War ended in Russia's defeat and the continued enslavement of Bulgaria), some indefinable force will cut him down. The final pages of *On the Eve* contain lengthy though inconclusive ruminations on the meaning of death which cuts short such a significant life, ruminations grounded in the tension between Turgenev's innate philosophical nihilism and the optimism of a man with a goal, like Insarov. Turgenev could not himself believe with such dedication, but he admired those who could even though he was persuaded they were doomed to failure.

Nihilism as a political phenomenon rather than a philosophical one was central to Turgenev's next and finest novel, *Fathers and Sons* (more precisely, *Fathers and Children*). He

[25]

later wrote that he first conceived of the book upon meeting an unnamed provincial doctor who impressed him as representative of a particular social type which he then embodied in the novel's hero, Bazarov. Commencing work on the manuscript in October of 1860, he completed the first version about a year later, then spent the last months of 1861 revising the text and agonizing over whether he ought to publish it at all in view of the widespread political unrest among the peasantry and students following the emancipation of the serfs in the spring. But Katkov the editor knew a good novel when he saw one—he published Tolstoy and Dostoevsky as well as Turgenev—and substantially decided the matter for him, bringing it out in the February, 1862, issue of the *Russian Herald*. In the summer of that year it appeared in a separate edition, with the addition of a dedication to Belinsky.

Fathers and Sons was composed for at least two major purposes: to contrast representatives of the best in the older and younger generations; and to demonstrate that the idealistic theories of the young, however admirable in the abstract, could not withstand confrontation with the realities of life.

The ideological standard-bearer of the older generation is Pavel Petrovich Kirsanov. An Anglophile and a man of cultivation, Pavel is also a bachelor embittered by a long-term enslavement of passion to a captious and mysterious princess. In his mouth Turgenev placed the major tenets of his own generation: a belief in principles as a guide to action; admiration of civilization and its accomplishments coupled with a denial that anything essential can be accomplished by brute force; a conviction that an enlightened aristocracy is essential for the well-being of the nation; respect for the proprieties and customs of social intercourse. His opponent, Bazarov, the primary representative of the younger generation, resembles him in many

[26]

facets of his emotional and psychological make-up but differs from him sharply in his philosophical approach to life. Bazarov is the great "negator," the quintessential "nihilist" (though Turgenev did not invent the word, he gave it popularity as a tag for the political radicals of the 1860s). He denies any validity to existing customs and social structures, insisting that they be swept away and space cleared for something better to be built; he refuses to recognize received authorities and even scoffs at medicine, though he is studying to be a doctor; he denies that human beings possess any individuality, as for him they are simply "copies," constituent parts of a social collective; he tends to equate evil with illness, which can be eliminated by altering the social order; he lacks any appreciation of art and aesthetics generally. Philosophically he is a thorough materialist. The intellectual clashes between Pavel Petrovich and Bazarov, intensified by their instinctive personal dislike for each other, constitute an important part of the book. Essentially these are debates rather than discussions. Since neither is genuinely willing to listen to the other, no meeting of minds occurs, but Bazarov usually bests his opponent because he is quite willing to push his arguments to their logical extreme upon provocation, whereupon Pavel Petrovich can only gape. Later on the enmity between them results in a duel, which Bazarov wins, physically and also spiritually, by magnanimously binding his opponent's wounds.

But if Bazarov gains the philosophical battle with Pavel Petrovich, and through him with the older generation as a whole, he loses the struggle with life. The very duel with Pavel Petrovich supplies an example of this: though Bazarov in theory rejects the notion of honor and dueling as a social institution, when he is actually challenged his pride causes him to accept the duel. The clearest instance of the failure of his doctrines to

[27]

bear up under the testing of real life is his love for Odintsova, the book's beautiful but cold heroine who does not mind flirting with him so long as the involvement does not become serious and disrupt her placid routine. Bazarov thinks love solely a matter of physiology: if one cannot "achieve one's aim" with one woman, drop her and find another. And in fact it is Odintsova's physical beauty which first attracts him: a physical lust akin to malice drives him to make his confession of love to her. But when Odintsova refuses him, Bazarov to his own amazement discovers that he cannot put her out of his mind. He keeps coming back to her in the hope that she may relent, and at the end summons her to his deathbed to bid her farewell. In this and other ways Bazarov partially falls prey to the "romanticism" of which he is so contemptuous. His theory of sexual attraction turns out to be invalid.

After love, death is the final irrational factor Bazarov had not reckoned with. Like Insarov, he is felled before he actually accomplishes anything: while dissecting a corpse he cuts himself and falls ill because no disinfecting substance is immediately available. Before the conclusion he grasps more clearly the mysteries of existence. "Yes," says the great negator on his deathbed, "just try to negate death. It negates you instead, and that's all there is to it."

After *Fathers and Sons* appeared, the question of the author's intent in writing it was paramount in the minds of the radical literary critics who discussed it. Dmitri Pisarev and his journal *Russian Word* argued that Turgenev had simply tried to be objective in picturing the younger generation, and that a young person should be quite pleased with Bazarov's portrayal. To be sure, Turgenev had included the figures of Sitnikov and Kukshina, two intellectual and moral travesties of Bazarov, but it had to be admitted that such people as these actually existed in reality and did no credit to the radical movement. Pisarev thus felt that there was nothing intentionally "anti-nihilist," or deliberately directed against the young radicals, in the book. But the other and more influential segment of the radical intelligentsia, led by Chernyshevsky and Dobrolyubov's heir Maksim Antonovich, assailed Turgenev vigorously for having slandered the younger generation, declaring that, since he stood revealed as such a reactionary, all his previous novels should be consigned to oblivion. When Turgenev visited St. Petersburg in the spring of 1862, he found to his dismay that those he considered his enemies welcomed him, while those he would have liked to think were his allies scorned him. Some, he later recalled sadly, had informed him then that they had burned photographs of him "with a haw-haw of contempt." In April of 1862 Turgenev wrote a lengthy letter to a group of Russian students at Heidelberg University defending his creation of Bazarov, proclaiming in the standard political idiom that his entire work was directed "against the gentry as the dominant class," and throwing up his hands at the students' claim that the idiotic Kukshina was his most successful character. But such was the intellectual atmosphere in Russia at that time that all his protestations availed him little.

The decade of the 1860s was a sharp-edged but seminal one in Russian intellectual history. The hopes aroused by Alexander II's accession to power were crowned by the emancipation of the serfs in 1861 and lesser but still important reforms, as of the courts, in immediately subsequent years. But Chernyshevsky, Dobrolyubov, Pisarev, and their allies, the descendants of the philosophical radicals of the 1840s, were not content with even these substantial changes: they went on to demand much more. The agitation for drastic change reached a crescendo in 1862, after the radicals had denounced the emancipation as a hoax, but it was quelled in that year through such actions as the suspension of *The Contemporary* and *Russian Word*, the imprisonment of Chernyshevsky and Pisarev, and most especially the outbreak of a rebellion in Poland in early 1863, which rallied public opinion to the government's side. Thereafter, deciding that the arson and university closing of 1861–62 had served little purpose, those hard-core radicals who were prepared to give their lives for the cause embarked upon a course of individual terrorism against high government officials. A deflected shot fired in April of 1866 at Alexander II in the heart of St. Petersburg inaugurated the era dominated by assassins and bomb-throwers, an era which culminated in the successful assassination of Alexander fifteen years later but which continued sporadically into the twentieth century. It is these terrorists, most of whom paid with their lives for their deeds, who were called "nihilists" by Western Europeans in the 1870s and 1880s.

The relations between the old-style liberals like Turgenev and the younger generation of the 1860s were delicate at best. Turgenev felt nearer to the radical than the conservative camp; he took pains to cultivate the young radicals, explain his attitudes to them, and attain some sort of understanding with them. But in the 1860s they for the most part would not have him, and he was compelled willy-nilly to ally himself with the more conservative elements of the Russian literary world, publishing in their chief organ, *Russian Herald*, during most of the decade. He could not condone the violence and terrorism perpetrated by the radicals, but at the same time he remained convinced that they were essentially correct in their outlook. Thus it was that many years later, in a brief prose poem, Turgenev wrote sadly of his attempts to tell the truth, only to be met with disdain from "honorable souls." All he could do, he felt, was continue on his path and hope that eventually he would be understood. "Pummel me, but be healthy and well-fed" was the slightly masochistic way he put it.

The unexpectedly violent reaction to *Fathers and Sons* gave rise to significant literary consequences for Turgenev. Indeed, for about a year after its publication he wrote virtually nothing of consequence. Then he reappeared bearing an odd concoction, begun some years before, entitled "Phantoms." When he printed it at the beginning of 1864 in a new journal edited by Dostoevsky, he went to great lengths to emphasize its apolitical character, subtitling it "A Fantasy" and equipping it with a brief introduction in which he asked the reader to take it at face value and not read anything into it. "Phantoms" is a series of disjointed sketches with an anonymous narrator whisked about nocturnally by a supernatural being called Ellis. Ellis is able to transport him at will not only through space but also through time: for example, she shows him Julius Caesar's legions marching in the days of imperial Rome's glory. During one of these nightly episodes, however, Ellis is attacked by a mysterious creature the narrator recognizes as death. He recovers consciousness lying on the ground near a beautiful woman, who embraces him passionately and promptly vanishes. One of the few minor items Turgenev wrote in the years following "Phantoms" was another series, this time of brief ruminations, entitled "Enough" (1865) and subtitled "Passages from a Dead Artist's Notes." "Enough" is Turgenev at his sentimental and self-pitying worst, consisting as it does of meditations on melancholy themes of lost happiness, the indifference of nature, the inevitability of destruction and the void, all done in a mood redolent of Schopenhauer. The work ends with a Shakespearean quotation in English: "The rest is silence."

Though this retreat from literature was only temporary (among his friends his repeated declarations of intent to abandon literature forever became something of a joke, and Dostoevsky used them to embarrassing effect in his nasty caricature of Turgenev as Karmazinov in *The Possessed*), his experiences of 1862 did alter the "mix" of his writing significantly. To be sure, he wrote two more novels, but they now appeared less frequently—whereas he published four between 1855 and 1862, he put out only two from 1862 to 1877—and the relative importance of the "mysterious" or the "supernatural" in his fiction increased. Turgenev did not believe in God, and superficially it might seem he would be little interested in supernatural phenomena. Yet he was haunted by a suspicion that there was something more to life than meets the physical eye. In 1864 he composed a small story entitled "The Dog," in which he described something that may have been an apparition—but then may have had a natural explanation too. He ventured no answer to the question with which he began and concluded the story: "But if we allow the possibility of the supernatural, the possibility of its intrusion into real life, . . . then what role is left for common sense?" "Knock. . .Knock. . .Knock" (1870), set in the romantic 1830s, is written in a similar vein. Its hero, Lieutenant Teglev, appears to others to be a "fatal" type who bears the seal of a man of destiny (in speaking of him, the narrator makes the interesting comment that a belief in fate is equivalent to a belief in the "significance of life"). Each of the individual occurrences in the chain leading to Teglev's decision to take his own life has a completely natural explanation, but the way in which they combine is at the very least mysterious: the over-all pattern seems "fated," although at one point Teglev must do some forcing to fit a major event into the pattern. Here, as in "The Dog," Turgenev left himself a way out so that he would not have to commit himself irrevocably to the proposition that the supernatural does play a role in human life.

As the 1860s wore on, Turgenev began a return to the political novel, and his last two novels were even more political than the first four. He began writing *Smoke* around the end of 1865, dropped it for a time, then published it in early 1867 in the *Russian Herald* despite some disagreements over it with Katkov. Curiously enough, this work is built around a love affair of a typically Turgenevian stripe, but one in which the man, Litvinov, is determinedly and avowedly apolitical. Turgenev masterfully develops the love conflict around the question of whether Litvinov will succeed in wrenching his beloved, Irina, from the stifling world of Russian high society in which she is embedded in the German resort town of Baden-Baden, or whether she will enslave him with chains of passion and make of him a "kept man" to whom she can repair for surcease from the banality of the social circles in which she moves. In the end she proves too weak, too permeated by the poisons which have circulated about her for so many years, to leave her husband and his social milieu and follow Litvinov; and since Litvinov is exceptionally strong among Turgenev's heroes and demands all or nothing from her, the two part. At the novel's conclusion it is for once the woman who has missed her opportunity and become embittered, while Litvinov is able to renew his relationship with his former fiancée.

The political aspects of *Smoke* are treated in conjunction with Litvinov and his love affair, though he is more an observer of political discussion than a participant in it. Turgenev delineates with acid pen the generals, high bureaucrats, and stultified nobility who constitute Irina's circle and who are incapable of a single original or even intelligent thought. In many cases he denies them the dignity of full names, designating them by initials. Even the tolerant Litvinov can find no redeeming features in them. The opposite end of the political spectrum is represented by the members of the Gubarev circle,

[33]

which Litvinov visits on occasion. Though they waste their time in pointless wrangling, and though many of them eventually return to Russia and become petty despots, Turgenev feels that they are not really bad people at heart, but simply misguided ones. The rightist and leftist groups resemble each other in a number of ways, but their creator is noticeably more inclined toward the latter.

Turgenev advanced many of his own favorite notions through an admirable but weak character in *Smoke*, Potugin. Potugin is what Litvinov is in danger of becoming: a man so helplessly in love with Irina that he trails about after her to do her bidding. In lengthy conversations (or monologues, to put it more precisely) with Litvinov, Potugin sets forth his political and philosophical views, as, for instance, that Russia has contributed nothing to the progress of mankind and that Western civilization holds the only promise for Russia's future development. Potugin believes firmly in the West, but without rejecting his homeland even though he sees it in a jaundiced light.

In view of Turgenev's "plague on both your houses" political approach in *Smoke*, it is not astonishing that he was reviled from all sides for it. Members of the establishment resented being pictured as empty-headed reactionaries, and the radicals took offense at the depiction of the Gubarev circle, which was in fact one of Turgenev's most "antinihilist" creations. Pisarev, the chief radical critic still on the scene at the time, continued to display understanding for Turgenev, but even he criticized him for abandoning the line he had followed in creating Bazarov, and turning instead to such a socially insignificant hero as Litvinov.

During the bulk of the 1860s, from 1864 to 1870, Turgenev resided near the Viardots in Baden-Baden. He made an average of one trip a year to Russia to keep abreast of developments, but fundamentally he was now living abroad and merely visiting his homeland. Toward the end of the decade the political situation in Russia eased noticeably, so at that time he published his reminiscences of Belinsky as well as a series of comments "On the Subject of *Fathers and Sons*," in which he fell victim to the compulsion felt by many of the "antinihilist" novelists to justify their books, so badly "misunderstood" by their readers. Ordinarily these efforts did their authors little good, and Turgenev was no exception to the rule.

If Turgenev was at his most Slavophilic in the later 1850s, while writing *A Nest of Gentlefolk*, he was at his most Slavophobic at the conclusion of the 1860s. He was a European, he used to say then, and not particularly a Russian: "so bin Ich . . . ganz und gar Deutsch" ("I am totally and completely German"), he wrote to a correspondent in 1870. It is thus the more ironic that the conflict of that same year between France and Germany, the two great bearers of Western civilization, drove him from his European nest: after the outbreak of hostilities the Viardots, being French citizens, had to leave Germany, and Turgenev followed them, first to London, then to France. And it was in France that the Russian-German lived from then on.

During the 1870s, while residing in France and continuing to pay occasional visits to Russia, Turgenev maintained relationships with certain of the greatest French writers of that day on a footing of at least equality, and sometimes superiority. He wrote and spoke French and German with native fluency and could handle English with some competence, a rare accomplishment for a nineteenth-century Russian. His vast correspondence, which has only recently been brought together in something resembling its entirety, was conducted in any one of four languages, and contains an immense mass of interesting commentary on contemporary literary and political events.

[35]

Henry James, who first met Turgenev in 1875, declared him "the richest, the most delightful, of talkers," and found him and his work fascinating, although he was grieved that evidently Turgenev had no such high opinion of his, James's, writing. At the same time, as James emphasized in his memoirs of Turgenev, he was not at all gallicized: "No sojourner in Paris was less French than he," James recalled. And indeed the brothers Goncourt record in their journal, not only samples of Turgenev's stimulating table-talk, but also the fact that he discoursed mostly about Russia and things Russian. All of this speaks of the ambivalence of his character: in Russia he was a European, in Europe a Russian.

Turgenev's closest literary associates in Paris included Daudet, Flaubert, and Zola. Daudet recollected first meeting Turgenev at Flaubert's. Daudet being unusual among Frenchmen in that he was familiar with Turgenev's work, and Turgenev being unusual among authors in that he loved music, the two had much in common. Turgenev and Zola also got along well—Turgenev evidently had a hand in arranging for him to write a series of articles for the leading Russian liberal monthly, *Herald of Europe*, between 1875 and 1880—but there must have been some powerful temperamental differences between them. Thus the Goncourts record that once the two quarreled about love: Zola maintained that the only thing special about this emotional state was the prospect of copulation, while Turgenev argued that it was an extraordinary phenomenon distinct from its material and physiological aspects. Temperamentally Turgenev was probably closest to Flaubert in these years. He spent many evenings in conversation at his home, and their friends felt the two almost made a couple, with Turgenev playing the feminine role. Daudet commented that sometimes in nature "feminine souls are embodied in titanic forms" (Turgenev was a man of large build), and James remarked that Turgenev and Flaubert each "had a tender regard for the other," mixed with some compassion for Flaubert on Turgenev's part.

At the very time when Turgenev was living abroad and consorting so extensively with foreigners, however, in his writing he manifested a deep interest in peculiarly Russian themes. In "A Strange Story" of 1869 he describes a mad wandering Holy Fool attended by a girl of good family who has found in him a leader before whom she can humiliate herself. Though he does not sympathize with the form it has taken, Turgenev cannot help admiring the strength of her devotion. "A King Lear of the Steppes," a long short story published in 1870 and since unduly neglected by students of Russian literature, is extraordinarily Russian in its execution despite the fact that it takes its title and plot idea from English literature. The hero of the story is a landowner named Kharlov, a man of immense build and of undisputed authority over his two daughters, their husbands, and his peasants. But when he sees in a dream a black foal which he interprets as a symbol of impending death, he resolves to distribute his earthly goods to his heirs before his demise, confident that they will continue to revere him as before even without any material motive for doing so. Unhappily, he is mistaken, for once they obtain title to his property his heirs gradually deprive him of what little he has retained until finally they drive him from the estate altogether. Up to this point Kharlov's pride has kept him from complaining, but an almost chance remark arouses his rage: what he has created he can also destroy, he thinks to himself. In the concluding scene he mounts the roof of his former house and sets to wrecking it with his bare hands until he falls to the ground and injures himself so severely that he shortly dies. "A King Lear of the Steppes" is remarkable not only for the drama of its plot but also for its language, based on the colloquial style of the narrator and on peasant speech, and for its treatment of certain facets of the Russian character, not all of them positive.

Turgenev's interest in things Russian, however, did not submerge his internationalist approach. "Torrents of Spring" (1871), his lengthiest work aside from his novels, presents a Russian hero involved with an Italian heroine in a German setting (Frankfort and Wiesbaden) of thirty years before. Its plot is reminiscent of that of *Smoke*, although the hero, Sanin, is much weaker than Litvinov. It begins as something unusual for Turgenev, that is, an account of love apparently fulfilled, with Sanin meeting a crucial test of resolution that enables him eventually to win a promise of marriage from the beautiful Gemma against substantial obstacles. But precisely when the reader has been lulled into the belief that Turgenev is after all capable of picturing successful love, the author abruptly drops his hero into the abyss of abject enslavement to the most predatory heroine he ever created, Polozova. Polozova, a wealthy woman of peasant origin, finds meaning for her life solely by enslaving men through the power of lust: at the moment of her triumph over Sanin, "her eyes, wide and so light they seemed white, expressed nothing but pitiless insensitivity and the satiety of victory." As a result of Polozova's intervention, Sanin loses his self-respect as well as his fiancée, and ends as one of the most embittered of Turgenev's numerous stand of lonely, middle-aged bachelors. Life, he muses to himself in the introduction, is not so much a stormy sea as a calm one with transparent waters. But beneath this superficially benign surface are many mysteries and many evils: on the "dark, slimy bottom" there are "hideous monsters," "all life's infirmities, sicknesses, griefs, insanity, poverty, blindness," any one of which may at any moment rise to the surface and capsize the boat in which the observer floats. The catastrophic shift

[38]

in Sanin's fortunes illustrates this, and there is much in "Torrents of Spring" to justify Turgenev's referring to it as an "abortion" and remarking to a correspondent that he had conceived of it as full of blue sky and the song of larks, but it had turned out a poisonous toadstool: "I have never been so immoral," he added. The novelette, as it were, took on an evil life of its own under the author's pen.

Turgenev's sixth and last novel, *Virgin Soil*, appeared in early 1877 in the *Herald of Europe*. He worked over it for many years, composing thumbnail biographies of chief characters for his own use, but this did not guarantee the success of the final product, artistically the weakest of his novels. Evidently his prolonged residence in Western Europe and his lack of contact with Russian reality sapped the vitality of an art which sought to deal with contemporary times. The critics condemned *Virgin Soil* roundly upon its publication, and the verdict of later generations has not been appreciably more generous.

Virgin Soil is the most political of Turgenev's novels, being an attempt to trace the early history of the "movement to the people," which began about 1868. The "movement to the people" was based on the notion that radical students and intellectuals should conduct propaganda and agitation among the peasantry in order to make them a revolutionary force. But the ideas which the young people preached were too foreign to the outlook of the peasantry, and the entire movement proved a fiasco. Turgenev wrote *Virgin Soil* largely to demonstrate how and why the radicals failed despite their good intentions.

The book's principal hero is Aleksey Nezhdanov, who comes from an established family: his father was a high-ranking officer, and he has been given a first-rate education by a strict Swiss schoolmaster. His very inner being is aristocratic, moreover: his fine facial features are an external reflection of his love of the beautiful and his sensitive intellect. One of his major weaknesses as a revolutionary is a tendency to write poetry, an inclination he carefully conceals after joining the radical movement. The novel's climax occurs when he sallies forth in peasant clothing to enlighten the common people, only to discover that he cannot "simplify" himself to the degree required for this, and that furthermore he cannot overcome his instinctive aversion to some nasty peasant traits. The conflict between his inborn instincts and his intellectual convictions leads to self-destruction, in one of the few instances where a Hamlet-like Turgenevian personage goes so far as to take his own life. In Nezhdanov's personality the ideal enters into an irreconcilable contradiction with the real.

There are those in *Virgin Soil* who remain faithful to the cause, however: the plain-looking Mashurina, who loves Nezhdanov with an unrequited love, and the energetic Markelov, who also discovers it is no simple matter to conduct agitation among the peasantry. A species of ideological barometer in the novel is Marianna Sinetskaya, who deserts her guardian's home to run away with Nezhdanov but refuses to marry him until he commits himself totally to her. This Nezhdanov cannot bring himself to do, but by means of a letter written before his suicide he joins her with the character offered as the book's positive hero, Solomin. Solomin, a practical man who operates along English lines, manages a factory on his estate. He springs from the common people and is not a great talker, but he displays "common sense" in his judgments. Turgenev clearly hoped the future would belong to him.

The radical critics, however, violently disputed Turgenev's assessment of the class to which the future might belong, and he, as usual, attempted to mollify them by agreeing with them as far as he could. But they would not be placated despite the novel's satirical thrusts against the aristocratic establishment. These were embodied especially in the person of Kollomeytsev, a pseudo-Westernizer who, though outwardly charming and graceful, is in fact a cruel exploiter of his peasants and a deep-dyed reactionary. Another despicable personage is Valentina Mikhaylovna Sipyagina, reminiscent of such predatory Turgenevian females as Natalya Petrovna (*A Month in the Country*) in her rivalry with her ward, and of Polozova ("Torrents of Spring") in her desire to bind the naïve Nezhdanov to herself by the bonds of love in order to inflate her own ego. Still, the love-intrigue, though important, is relatively less central in *Virgin Soil* than in any of the other novels.

Turgenev received honors as well as abuse in the latter half of the 1870s. In 1875 he settled for what remained of his life at Bougival near Paris, not far from the Viardots. He continued his excursions to Russia, as in the late summer of 1878 when he smoothed over his quarrel with Tolstoy and visited the latter's estate at Yasnaya Polyana. But he made his most triumphal return to his homeland during a visit to St. Petersburg and Moscow during the first months of 1879. At this time he was extensively feted by his fellow liberals in Russian society, and responded with pleasure to the evidences of his popularity among the reading public. Shortly thereafter, in June of 1879, he journeyed to England to receive the honorary degree of Doctor of Civil Law from Oxford University, a token of esteem from a nation he esteemed, and which he therefore cherished.

Almost exactly one year later, in June of 1880, Turgenev participated in ceremonies connected with the unveiling of a monument to the great Russian poet Alexander Pushkin in Moscow. The festivities of 1880 remain as one of the outstanding public occasions in the history of Russian literature. Many leading writers were in attendance, and Dostoevsky in particular delivered the most famous speech of his career then. Turgenev chose to be cautious in defining Pushkin's place in Russian letters. He was ready to dub him the first "poet-artist" in Russian literature, he was willing to acknowledge him as the synthesizer of Russian literary language, but he would not crown him the "national poet" in the same sense in which Shakespeare and Goethe were considered the national poets of their respective homelands. Such ambiguity, however honest it may have been intellectually, did not suit the tenor of the occasion.

After the publication of *Virgin Soil* Turgenev's relatively sparse production was limited to short pieces. "A Desperate Character" of 1881 presents an absorbing analysis of a certain type of personality which cannot stand the proprieties of staid bourgeois society and seems desperately bent on its own destruction. "The Song of Triumphant Love," also dating from 1881, is unusual in that it is set in sixteenth-century Ferrara instead of contemporary Russia or Russia of the recent past, and in that it deals with plainly supernatural occurrences, though in the form of a legend, connected with an unsuccessful love. A unique treatment of the theme of love and death is offered in "After Death (Klara Milich)," written in 1882, the last full year of the author's life. The hero, a sensitive, lonely young man named Aratov, arouses the love of a singer and actress, Klara Milich, though they have never met at the time. A strong-willed character who has promised to "take" the man she loves if she ever encounters him, she commits suicide on stage after an abortive attempt to bring Aratov to her feet during an interview in Moscow. Having failed to conquer him in this world, she returns to capture him in the next: Aratov falls in love with her after her death, sees her in dreams and visions, and ends by passing blissfully through the gate of death to join her. "Klara Milich" is one of Turgenev's most powerful statements on the exceptional nature of love, which can overcome the grave.

At the twilight of his writing career Turgenev effected something of a return to the poetic attempts of his first years in the *Poems in Prose*, brief lyrical vignettes on various subjects of usually not more than a page, and sometimes only a few lines. Written at different times between 1878 and 1882, each of them is carefully dated. Though frequently oversentimental, they do treat many themes which had long been constants in Turgenev's work, and at the very least they are instructive as indices to his thinking in those years. Certain of them embody distillations of a philosophy of life derived from many years of observation of mankind's weaknesses and related to the capsule one-sentence aphorisms on human behavior with which he studded his novels and stories from the beginning, and some of which could be quite cynical. Philosophically speaking, however, the center of gravity of the *Poems in Prose* lies not in such vignettes as these but in pieces on more serious, usually very pessimistic, subjects. One theme is the indifference of nature to human aspirations, which early received notable expression in the introduction to his "Excursion to the Woodlands" of 1857: in the presence of the great forest, Turgenev wrote then, man "feels that the last of his brothers might vanish from the face of the earth, and not a single needle on these pine branches would twitch." Similarly, in "Conversation" the Jungfrau and the Finsteraarhorn look down distantly upon the world below them at intervals of thousands of years and express their satisfaction when the frenzied activities of antlike humans in the lowlands cease and all is frozen and quiet. When the narrator inquires of personified nature in "Nature" what she is turning her attention to at that moment, she replies that she is strengthening the muscles of the flea so that he may more easily escape his

[43]

enemies. To the narrator's protestations about human values, she remarks that she cherishes humans no more and no less than any other of her creatures. One of the few prose poems with a religious coloration is "Christ," in which Jesus is perceived as a man with a face "like all other human faces," who by implication incorporates everything human within himself.

Two of the most famous sketches from the *Poems in Prose* deal with Russia and her domestic political situation. "The Threshold" points up both the dedication of the Russian revolutionaries and Turgenev's ambiguous attitude toward them. Questioned before being permitted to pass through a door, a girl says she is ready to die herself or commit a crime, that she even realizes she may one day lose faith in the cause to which she now dedicates herself. As she enters then, two voices accompany her, the first crying "Fool!" as the second responds "Saint!" In "The Russian Language," dated June, 1882, Turgenev found moral sustenance in the tongue of which he was such a master: "In days of doubt, in days of gloomy meditation upon the fate of my homeland—you alone are my strength and support, oh great, mighty, honest and free Russian language! Were it not for you how could we help despairing over everything done at home? But one must believe that such a language can only have been given to a great people!"

The most persistent theme in the prose poems, however, is that of death. It is central to the reminiscence of Turgenev's last meeting with Nekrasov. Its inevitability and unexpectedness are underlined in "The Old Woman" and "Tomorrow." It is treated allegorically in "The Insect," a tableau of a crowded hall into which flies a large and menacing insect. Everyone sees it and retreats from it in horror except its victim, who expires when it stings him on the forehead. The stolid resignation or deep despair of the common people when faced with the death of loved ones is the subject of two sketches. But in two others, both of them for some reason associated with sparrows, Turgenev sounds a note of hope or defiance: in "We Will Still Put Up a Fight" he draws inspiration from the cocky cheerfulness displayed by a family of sparrows while far above them circles the hawk who can destroy them at any time he chooses; and in "The Sparrow" the mother bird's readiness to defend her young against an immense dog causes Turgenev to meditate: "Love, I thought, is stronger than death and the fear of death. Life maintains itself and develops only through that, through love."

Turgenev had long been preoccupied with death, of course. It had concerned him in some of his earliest works, and once in 1872, while discoursing at Flaubert's, he commented that he had always somehow been surrounded by "an odor of death, of non-being, of dissolution," a death which he defined as the inability to love. The predominance given the subject in the *Poems in Prose* become immediately relevant to his life when he fell seriously ill in April of 1883. From that time on the die was cast, though he experienced periods of temporary improvement. He continued his literary work when he could, publishing some new pieces and laboring over an edition of his collected writings, but death, however imagined — as a black foal in "King Lear of the Steppes," the more conventional skulls in one of the *Poems in Prose*, or a monkeylike creature huddled in a boat and holding a flask of dark liquid in a striking dream of Aratov's in "Klara Milich" — would not forever be denied. On September 3, 1883, Turgenev died at Bougival after an extremely painful illness. "His end," Henry James wrote, "was not serene and propitious, but dark and almost violent." This remark points to depths within Turgenev which he himself could not plumb to the bottom, though he was aware of their existence.

SELECTED BIBLIOGRAPHY

NOTE: *The first serious attempt to collect all of Turgenev's works and letters has just been completed in the Soviet Union. The task of gathering together his correspondence, scattered all over Europe and America, was truly a formidable one, and 15 volumes were required to print all the letters that have so far been discovered. His collected fiction takes up 15 volumes as well.*

The indefatigable Constance Garnett long ago rendered the bulk of Turgenev's writing into English: The Novels of Ivan Turgenev *(including his short stories) (15 vols.; London, Heinemann, 1894–99). The currently most easily available selected edition in English, though poorly translated and not very extensive, is the* Vintage Turgenev *(2 vols.; New York, Vintage Books, 1960).*

Critical Works and Commentary

Brodianski, Nina. "Turgenev's Short Stories: A Revaluation," *Slavonic and East European Review,* XXXII, No. 78 (December, 1953), 70–91.

Carr, E. H. "Turgenev and Dostoevsky," *Slavonic Review,* VIII, No. 22 (June, 1929), 156–63.

Chamberlin, William Henry. "Turgenev: The Eternal Romantic," *Russian Review,* V, No. 2 (Spring, 1946), 10–23.

Folejewski, Zbigniew, "The Recent Storm Around Turgenev as a Point in Soviet Aesthetics," *Slavic and East European Journal,* VI, No. 1 (Spring, 1962), 21–27.

Freeborn, Richard. Turgenev: The Novelist's Novelist. New York, 1960.

Garnett, Edward. Turgenev: A Study. London, 1917.

Gettman, Royal. Turgenev in England and America. Urbana, Ill., 1941.

Howe, Irving. "Turgenev: The Politics of Hesitation," in Politics and the Novel, pp. 114–38. New York, 1957.

Kagan-Kans, Eva. "Fate and Fantasy: A Study of Turgenev's Fantastic Stories," *Slavic Review,* XVIII, No. 4 (December, 1969), 543–60.

Lerner, Daniel. "The Influence of Turgenev on Henry James," *Slavonic and East European Review,* XX, No. 1 (December, 1941), 28–54.

Lloyd, John A. T. Ivan Turgenev. London, 1942.

Magarshack, David. Turgenev: A Life. London, 1954.

Mandel, Oscar. "Molière and Turgenev: The Literature of No-Judgement," *Comparative Literature*, XI, No. 3 (Summer, 1959), 233–49.

Matlaw, Ralph. "Turgenev's Art in Spring Torrents," *Slavonic and East European Review*, XXXV, No. 84 (December, 1956), 157–71.

——"Turgenev's Novels: Civic Responsibility and Literary Predilection," *Harvard Slavic Studies*, IV (1957), 249–62.

Sayler, O. "Turgenieff as a Playwright," *North American Review*, CCXIV, No. 790 (September, 1921), 393–400.

Sergievsky, Nicholas N. "The Tragedy of a Great Love: Turgenev and Pauline Viardot," *American Slavic and East European Review*, V, No. 14–15 (November, 1946), 55–71.

Wilson, Edmund. "Turgenev and the Life-Giving Drop," in Ivan Turgenev, Literary Reminiscences and Autobiographical Fragments, pp. 3–64. Tr. David Magarshack. New York, 1958.

Woodcock, George. "The Elusive Ideal: Notes on Turgenev," *Sewanee Review*, LXIX, No. 1 (January–March, 1961), 34–47.

Woolf, Virginia. "The Novels of Turgenev," *Yale Review*, XXIII, No. 2 (Winter, 1934), 276–83.

Yachnin, Rissa, and David Stam. Turgenev in English: A Checklist of Works By and About Him. New York, 1962.

Yarmolinsky, Avrahm. Turgenev: The Man, His Art and His Age. New York, 1959.

37-300